The Anglo-Saxons

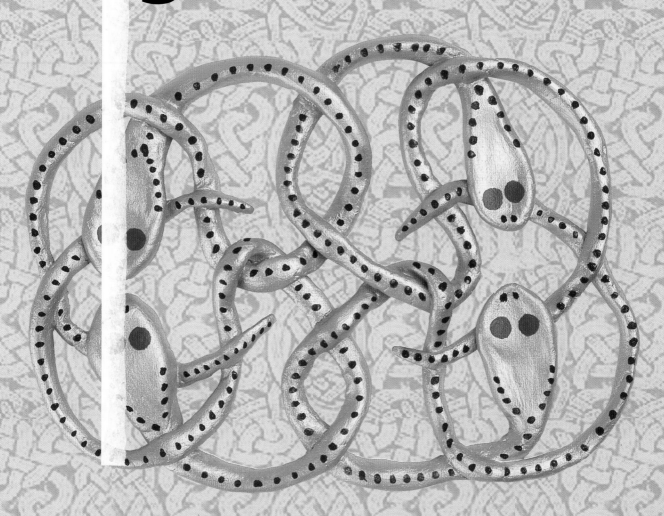

Written by Sally Hewitt

First published in 2006 by Franklin Watts
338 Euston Road, London NW1 3BH

Franklin Watts Australia
Level 17/207 Kent Street, Sydney NSW 2000

Copyright © Franklin Watts 2006

Editor: Rachel Tonkin
Designers: Rachel Hamdi and Holly Fulbrook
Picture researcher: Diana Morris
Craft models made by: Anna-Marie D'Cruz
Map artwork: Ian Thompson

Picture credits:
Bruce Adams/Eye Ubiquitous/Corbis: 8bl; Bargello Museum
Florence / Dagli Orti/Art Archive: 26c; Botin PL/Bridgeman Art
Library: 12br; © Trustees of the British Museum: 13b; The British
Library/Art Archive: 25t; The British Library/HIP/Topfoto: 7t,
24t; The British Museum/HIP/Topfoto: 11b, 26b; The British
Museum/Eileen Tweedy/ArtArchive: front cover t; Martyn
Chillmaid/Photographers Direct: 10; Mary Evans Picture Library:
13t; Museum of London/HIP/Topfoto: 8tr, 21t;
Picturepoint/Topfoto: 7b, 18b, 20b; Statens Historika Museum,
Stockholm/Werner Forman Archive: 22b; Topfoto: 11t, 12tl, 19t;
Charles Walker/Topfoto: 23t; Woodmansterne/Topfoto: 24b.

All other images: Steve Shott
With thanks to our model Reanne Khokhar

Every attempt has been made to clear copyright.
Should there be any inadvertent omission please
apply to the publisher for rectification.

A CIP catalogue record for this book
is available from the British Library

ISBN-13: 978 0 7496 6520 3
Dewey Classification: 942.01

Printed in China

Franklin Watts is a division of
Hachette Children's Books.

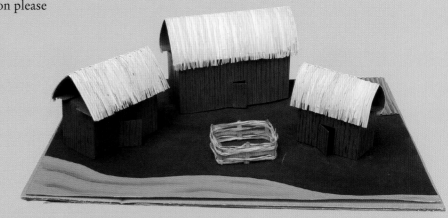

Contents

Invasion

The Angles, Saxons and Jutes were **tribes** who lived in northern Europe – what is now northern Germany, Denmark and northern Holland. They invaded Britain in the fifth and sixth centuries looking for better farmland where they could settle with their families.

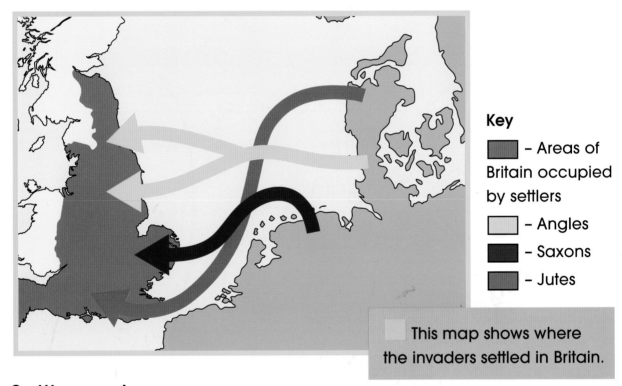

Key

◼ – Areas of Britain occupied by settlers

▢ – Angles

◼ – Saxons

◼ – Jutes

This map shows where the invaders settled in Britain.

Settlement

The invading tribes landed on the east and south coasts of Britain. They settled and gradually moved further and further inland. The settlers were known as the Anglo-Saxons and their language has become the English we speak today.

How do we know about the Anglo-Saxons?

The Anglo-Saxon Chronicle is a history of Britain written in Anglo-Saxon times. It gives us a year-by-year record of the lives of kings and bishops, of battles and other important events. Discoveries, such as the ship burial at Sutton Hoo, also tell us important things about the Anglo-Saxons.

A painting of King Alfred the Great (849–899). He ordered the Anglo-Saxon Chronicle to be written and kept up to date.

This is the impression left by the Sutton Hoo ship burial after the wood of the ship had rotted away.

Warriors

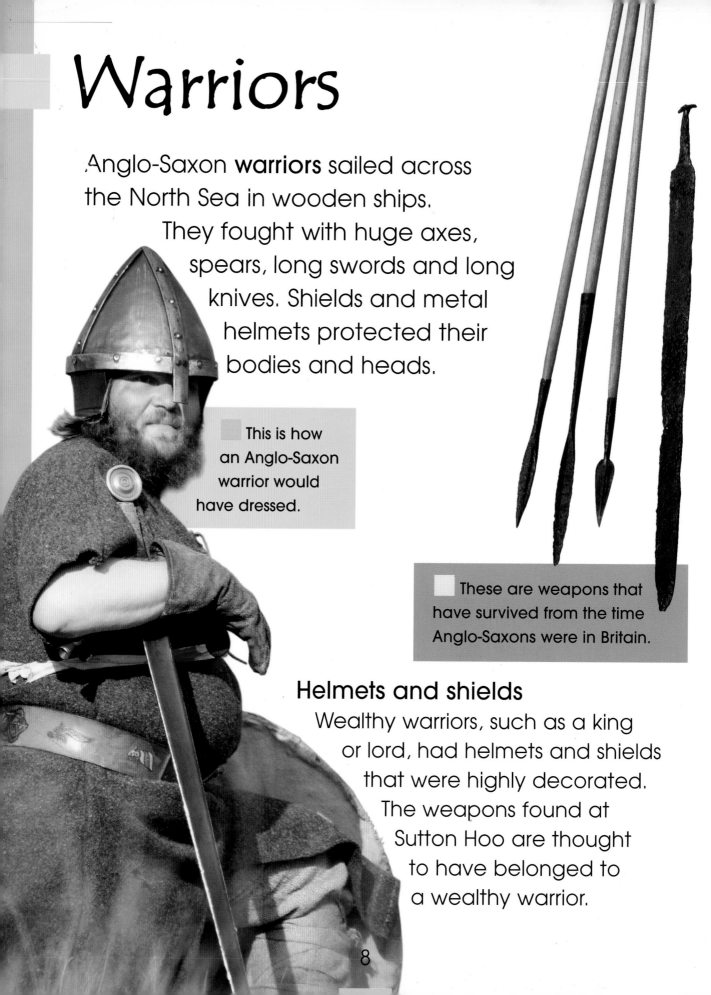

Anglo-Saxon **warriors** sailed across the North Sea in wooden ships. They fought with huge axes, spears, long swords and long knives. Shields and metal helmets protected their bodies and heads.

This is how an Anglo-Saxon warrior would have dressed.

These are weapons that have survived from the time Anglo-Saxons were in Britain.

Helmets and shields

Wealthy warriors, such as a king or lord, had helmets and shields that were highly decorated. The weapons found at Sutton Hoo are thought to have belonged to a wealthy warrior.

8

Warrior's shield

An ordinary warrior's shield was round. It was made from lime wood, which was light to carry, and covered in leather. It had a metal boss in the centre.

Make a shield

▶ 1 Cut a circle (30cm diameter) from a cardboard box and a strip of card about 30cm long. Bend the strip to make a handle and tape to the centre of the circle.

boss

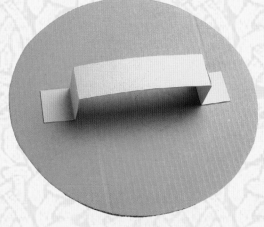

▶ 3 Paint a simple pattern onto your shield and a circle of brown paint around the outside.

▶ 2 To make the boss, cut a circle of metallic card (10cm diameter). Cut a line from the edge to the centre and bend into a flat cone. Snip at 2cm intervals around the edge to make it easy to stick to the centre of the shield.

Settlers

The Anglo-Saxon invaders built **settlements** and farmed the land. The settlements had a large hall in the centre surrounded by houses and workshops. Animals were kept in pens.

This is a hall in a **reconstruction** of an Anglo-Saxon village.

FELD field

TON village

WICK farm

FORD river crossing

LEIGH, LEY wood clearing

Place names

'Ham' was the Anglo-Saxon word for settlement, 'den' was a hill and 'worth' meant enclosed by a hedge. So the towns of Swaffham, Eversden and Boxworth in East Anglia were once Anglo-Saxon settlements.

Look out for Anglo-Saxon place names near where you live.

An Anglo-Saxon house was made of wood with a thatched roof. It had one big room where the family cooked, ate and slept. It had one door and a window which both faced south to catch the sun.

Make an Anglo-Saxon village

▶ **1** Use small boxes to make the base of each building. Draw a door 4cm wide and 3cm high on one side. Cut along one side and along the top and fold back the door.

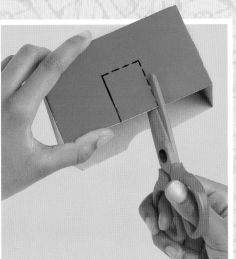

▶ **3** Paint the walls brown and add lines to look like wooden planks. Paint the roof to look like thatch (or stick on strips of raffia).Make a base from a piece of card and use raffia to make animal pens.

▶ **2** Fold rectangles of card in half lengthways for the roofs – the rectangle should be as long as each box.

Village life

Anglo-Saxon villagers all had jobs to do. The men hunted, fished, farmed and worked in the craft houses. Women spun and wove cloth, sewed and cooked. The children learnt by watching and helping their parents.

Food

Villagers kept cows, pigs, sheep and goats. Meat was only eaten on special occasions. They hunted rabbits, fished and gathered fruit, nuts and berries.

Cooking pots were hung over the fire, like this one in a reconstruction village.

Barley beer was drunk from drinking horns like this one.

Wheat, oats, rye and barley were grown and ground up to make bread.

Wild deer and boar were hunted by wealthy lords and kings.

Make a vegetable and barley stew

All these ingredients for an Anglo-Saxon vegetable stew could be grown in the nearby fields.

Ingredients

- 1 leek – peeled and sliced
- 1 onion – peeled and sliced
- 200g peas
- handful of chopped cabbage
- 200g (pearl) barley
- 1 bay leaf • pinch of sage
- pinch of salt

▶ **1** Put all the ingredients into a saucepan. Just cover with water and bring to the boil.

▶ **2** Turn the heat down and simmer for 40 minutes or until the barley is soft.

▶ **3** Take out the bay leaf. Ladle into a soup bowl and eat with a thick slice of bread.

Modern tips

Adapt your recipe for today and add some vegetable stock and a bit of cream!

Clothes

People made clothes from **linen** or wool. They spun sheep's wool into **yarn** and wove it into cloth. Dyes from plants were used to colour the cloth blue, yellow and red. Onion skins were used to dye clothes brown.

This woman and girl are wearing Anglo-Saxon costumes.

Anglo-Saxon men wore **tunics** and leggings. Women wore long dresses and head cloths. Their belts and shoes were made from leather. Children dressed like their parents.

Buckles and pins

Clothes were kept in place with buckles, pins and brooches. This beautiful buckle, found at Sutton Hoo, has a pattern of coiled snakes.

This gold buckle, found at Sutton Hoo, is very valuable.

Make a snake-design buckle

1 Roll out four sausages of air-hardening clay. Make them about 20cm long and flatten one end slightly to make the snakes' heads.

2 Arrange the four snakes in an **interweaving** pattern. Play around with the snakes until you are happy with your design. Then, squash the clay down where the snakes touch each other to fix in place.

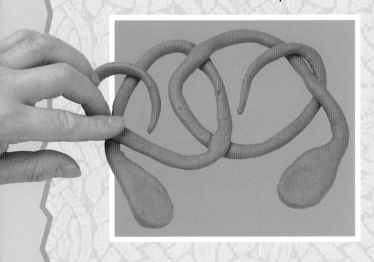

3 Leave in a safe place to dry out overnight.

4 When your buckle is dry, decorate with gold paint and black spots. Don't forget to paint on eyes.

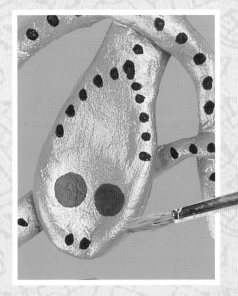

Storytellers

Anglo-Saxon storytellers travelled from village to village. They sang or recited their story poems from memory. The stories were about gods, kings and battles with brave heroes who fought monsters and dragons.

 Beowulf meets the dragon.

Beowulf

Beowulf is an exciting story about a hero called Beowulf who killed the terrible monster Grendel. He had many adventures until at last he was killed in a fight with a dragon. Only one original copy of the story of Beowulf, written down in the 11th century, still survives.

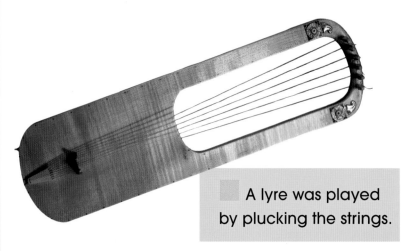

A lyre was played by plucking the strings.

Story-tellers played small instruments, such as harps, lyres and pipes. They were easy to carry around and could be used to add drama to their stories.

Make a lyre

▶ **1** Copy the shape of the lyre below onto card, making it about as big as this page. Ask an adult to help with cutting out the centre shape.

stick bridge here

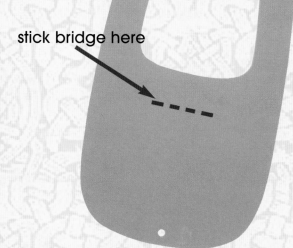

▶ **2** Punch six holes along the top and one hole centre bottom with a hole punch.

▶ **3** To make the bridge, fold a square of card (6 x 6cm) in half and fold back two flaps on each side. Snip six grooves along the top fold and stick to the lyre, as shown.

bridge

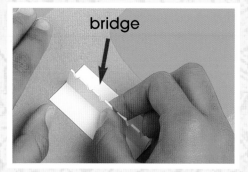

▶ **4** Cut six lengths of black thread about 40cm long. Thread each one through a hole at the top, over a groove in the bridge and through the bottom hole. Tie in place. Paint the lyre light brown and add gold decorations.

Death and burial

When the Anglo-Saxon invaders arrived in Britain, they brought their **pagan** religion with them. When they died, they were buried with things they might need in the **afterlife**.

Sutton Hoo

In 1939, an Anglo-Saxon ship burial was discovered at Sutton Hoo in Suffolk (see page 7). The man was buried in a wooden ship 24 metres long. We can learn about him from the possessions that were buried with him. Both pagan and Christian things were buried with him.

Many coins like these were found at Sutton Hoo.

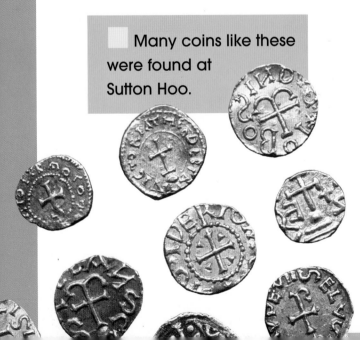

Things buried with Sutton Hoo man

Weapons and armour

An iron helmet stamped with pictures of battle scenes.

A huge shield with richly decorated fittings.

A mail-coat; an axe hammer; spears and a patterned sword.

Household goods

Silver dishes, cups and spoons.

Cooking pots.

Drinking horns.

Pastimes

A lyre.

An ivory piece for a game.

Jewellery

A gold buckle (see page 14) and clasps decorated with precious stones.

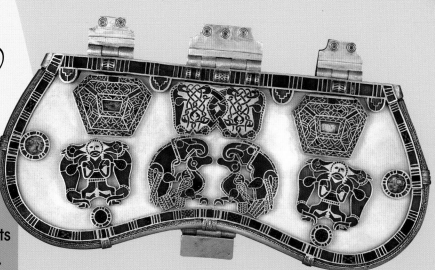

A purse lid from Sutton Hoo made with gold, garnets (precious stones) and glass.

Who was he?

▶ Write a story about the Sutton Hoo man.

Look at the things buried with him on this website:

www.thebritishmuseum.ac.uk/compass

Do you think he was a king, a soldier or a farmer? Was he wealthy or poor?

Sutton Hoo man was very important. He had lots of jewels and gold

▶ Draw a picture of what you think he looked like.

Kings and kingdoms

By AD 600, Anglo-Saxon Britain was divided into five main kingdoms – East Anglia, Mercia, Northumberland, Wessex and Kent.

Offa's Dyke

Offa was a powerful king of Mercia. In AD 787 he built a great ditch to protect his kingdom. It was 270 kilometres long. It is known as Offa's Dyke and you can still see it today running along the border between Wales and England.

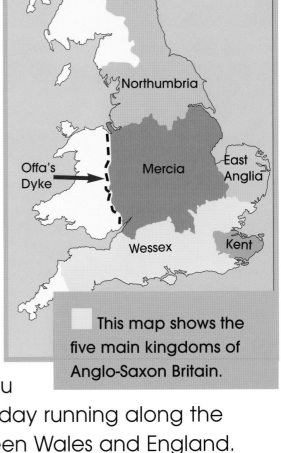

This map shows the five main kingdoms of Anglo-Saxon Britain.

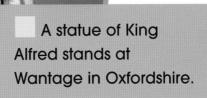

A statue of King Alfred stands at Wantage in Oxfordshire.

Alfred the Great

In AD 871, Alfred became king of Wessex. He is known as Alfred the Great. He fought against **Viking** invaders from Scandinavia and drove them out of his kingdom. The Vikings settled in the north east of what is now England.

The Anglo-Saxons used silver pennies for everyday buying and selling. These had pictures of the heads of kings, such as Offa and Alfred, stamped onto them.

This coin was made during King Alfred's reign. It is stamped with his head and his name. Letters on the other side spell the word London.

Design a coin

Design your own coin, pretending you were a rich king like Alfred.

▶ **1** Draw two circles on thick card bigger than a coin to give you room for your design.

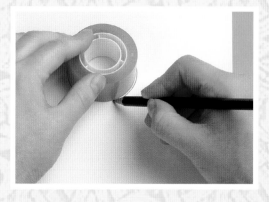

▶ **2** What will you put on each side? Look at some modern coins to give you ideas.

▶ **3** Decorate your coin with metallic paint and felt-tip pens.

What does your coin say about you?

Gods and goddesses

The Anglo-Saxon religion had many gods and goddesses.

Tiw was the god of war and justice among the gods.

Woden was the god of wisdom. He rode an eight-legged horse with wings.

Thor, god of thunder, had a hammer that came back to him after he threw it.

Frigg, goddess of marriage, was Woden's wife.

Days of the week

Can you work out which Anglo-Saxon god or goddess these weekdays are named after?

Friday

Tuesday

Wednesday

Thursday

(Answers are on page 29)

Pagan festivals

Some of the Christian festivals we celebrate today took the place of pagan festivals. Easter was the festival of Eostre, the goddess of Spring.

Easter eggs are given as a sign of new life.

Our **Harvest** Festival was the festival of Nerthus, the earth mother. A corn dolly was the symbol of Nerthus. Corn dollies, made from straw, were made to bring good luck in the next year.

A corn dolly in the shape of a crescent moon.

Make a corn dolly from art straws

▶ **1** Make three groups of three art straws.

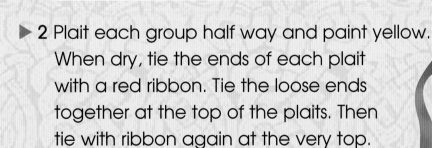

▶ **2** Plait each group half way and paint yellow. When dry, tie the ends of each plait with a red ribbon. Tie the loose ends together at the top of the plaits. Then tie with ribbon again at the very top.

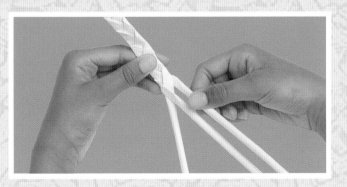

23

Monks and missionaries

In AD 597, the head of the Christian church Pope Gregory sent **missionaries** to Britain to convert the Anglo-Saxons to Christianity. A hundred years later, every British king was Christian.

The Lindisfarne **Gospels** were beautifully illustrated by monks at the monastery of Lindisfarne.

Monasteries

Churches and monasteries were built all over Britain. Monasteries were places of worship and learning where **monks** copied and illustrated books by hand and taught boys to read and write.

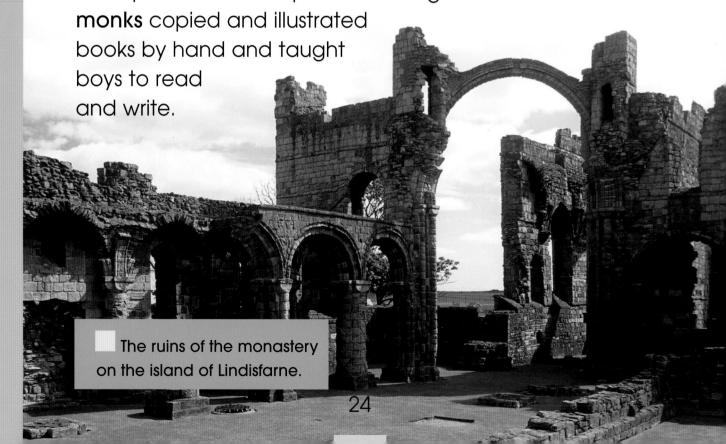

The ruins of the monastery on the island of Lindisfarne.

One famous monk was Saint Bede (673–735 CE). He wrote many important things in Latin including a chronicle of English history from the time of the Roman invasion. The Lindisfarne Gospels are thought to have been written and illustrated in 710–721 CE by just one monk, Eadfrith the Bishop of Lindisfarne.

Saint Bede at work at his desk in the monastery.

Decorated letters

Letters at the beginning of a page in the Lindisfarne Gospels were often decorated with pictures that illustrated the writing.

▶ Design and colour the letters of your initials.
What pictures could tell us something about you?

Runes and writing

Anglo-Saxon was originally written in letters called runes which were thought to have magic meanings. Runes were made up of straight lines. This made runes easier for people to carve.

The Anglo-Saxon Chronicle

The Anglo-Saxon Chronicle (see page 7) was written in Anglo-Saxon but instead of runes, the Roman alphabet was used. Today, English is written in the Roman alphabet.

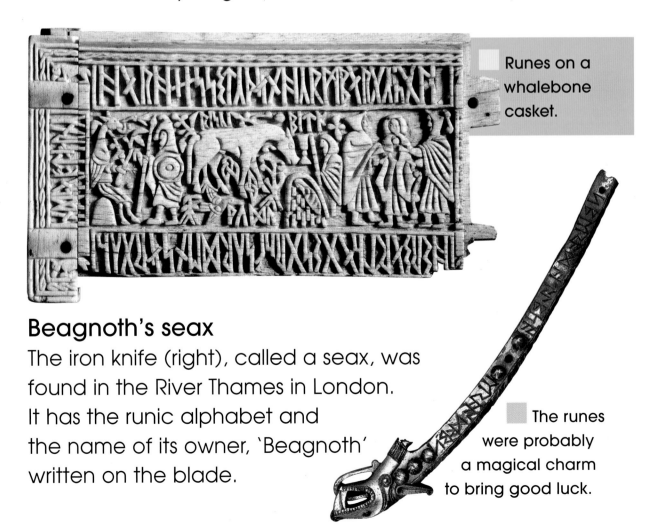

Runes on a whalebone casket.

Beagnoth's seax

The iron knife (right), called a seax, was found in the River Thames in London. It has the runic alphabet and the name of its owner, 'Beagnoth' written on the blade.

The runes were probably a magical charm to bring good luck.

Carve an Anglo-Saxon pattern

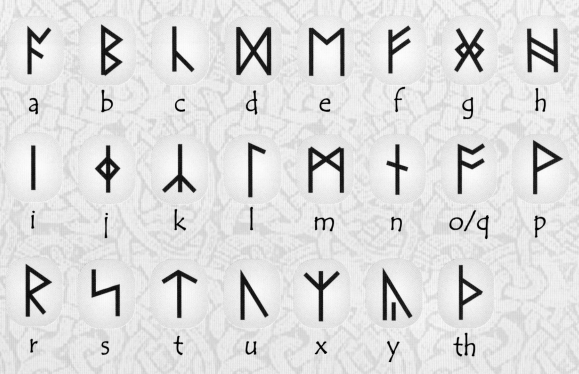

a	b	c	d	e	f	g	h
i	j	k	l	m	n	o/q	p
r	s	t	u	x	y	th	

▶ **1** Roll out a piece of air-drying clay until it is roughly 8mm thick. Cut out a square about 15cm x 15cm with a modelling knife.

▶ **2** Carve an Anglo-Saxon pattern onto the tile. Look in books or on the internet for ideas.

▶ **3** Decide what you want to write underneath it – your name, a place, a mysterious word. Work it out in runes on a piece of paper first.

Glossary

Afterlife

Anglo-Saxons believed in the afterlife – life after death. They were buried with things they would need in the afterlife.

Easter

The English name for the Christian spring festival to celebrate Jesus rising from the dead.

Festival

A celebration, such as a feast or a party, held on a special religious occasion.

Gospels

The first four books of the New Testament, part of the Christian Bible, telling of the life of Christ.

Harvest

The gathering of crops when they are ripe. Harvest festival is held in the Autumn.

Latin

The language spoken and written by the Romans.

Linen

Strong cloth made from the flax plant.

Loom

A machine for weaving cloth.

Missionary

A person sent to another country to persuade the people living there to change their religious beliefs.

Monk

A member of a religious community who lives and works in a monastery.

Pagan

A term used to describe religions where its followers worship many gods.

Reconstruction

A model of how something would have been in the past.

Settlement

A new place where people have decided to live.

Tribe

A group of people who live together who have the same background, religion and leader.

Tunic

A long top worn by an Anglo-Saxon man.

Vikings

Pirates and traders who came from Scandinavia.

Warriors

Soldiers who fight in battle.

Yarn

Wool twisted into a long thread that can be used for knitting and weaving.

Answer to question on page 22:

Tuesday – Tiw

Wednesday – Woden

Thursday – Thor

Friday – Frigg

Index